Flying While Brown

A-R Lingo

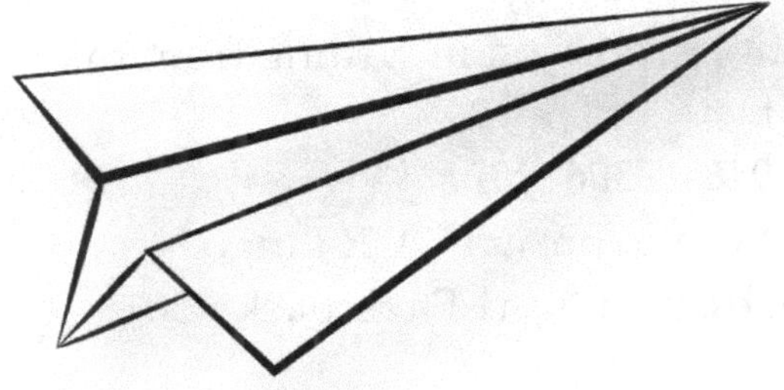

i

ISBN: *978-1720622871*
 Flying While Brown | A-R Lingo
Digital distribution | Paperback - 2018

Madison, WI

Dedication

To the past, present, and future.

To the underdog in the fight for freedom.

To the traveler, whether going home or leaving.

May your journey not be in vain.

Un

Itinerary, check. Passport, check. Laptop, camera, phone, all charged, packed with chargers, check, check, and check. Toothbrush and paste and spare boxers and socks, check. Duffle bag with some extra clothes and gifts, check. This must be the seventh or eighth time I make sure I have everything today. The excitement is almost too great to hold in! I've been looking forward to this moment for the past couple of weeks, and some two weeks they've been. Great, the shuttle's here; I should get going!

My family don't know I'm leaving tonight. I surprised them last time and I have everything in order to surprise them again, but since I know how this works now, I'm planning to spend the first night I'm back with Lamees before I go see them. I miss her the most. Zoo's going to pick me up from the airport once I land. I made sure he goes to the right terminal. He once got lost for an hour looking for me and I'm not going to let that get in my way this time. He should have the flowers and has agreed to keep my bags in his car and cover for me for the one night so that everything goes well. Man, I can't wait to be back.

It's a twenty-eight hour journey from my apartment in Wisconsin to the airport in Jeddah, and the jetlag is going to be horrendous, but I mean it's all worth it. I miss the food and the people and not being judged or talked to differently for looking like I do. Sure there are far less freedoms there, the society is generally backwards, and the heat is going to be annoying, but I've lived there for ten or so consecutive years and haven't stepped foot in the country in three. It's been so long and I can hardly wait.

The vehicle is a brand new Chrysler Town and Country and the driver seems nice. His name is Joshua and he compliments my bag saying it's nicer than most luggage he's hauled. He asks me where I'm from and where I'm headed. I tell him my story-I'm a Saudi student who's lived almost half his life all around the US and I'm going home for Christmas break after a long hiatus, although we don't really celebrate Christmas there. He tells me he's proud of me for persevering and that traveling is always exciting. Yeah, no kidding.

He tells me about this one time he got so tired of the mundaness of life and work and everything in the US. He decided to pack his bags and go to Spain for no reason, I find it noteworthy that he pronounces it "España." He thought he could use a break from the familiarity of the US and maybe teach English there for a year or two, any excuse to get out, really. His stories about learning colloquial Spanish are funny. One time he went to the market to buy some chicken and he mixed up the male and female words for the bird, so in a loud voice, he asked for Cock. Everyone around him went silent and the old lady next to him just shook her head in disapproval.

He says that it's important for people to travel; to spend at least a year in a land where they don't speak the language. To be in a place where as funny as you are, if your jokes don't translate well, your sense of humor is severely diminished and your ego is readjusted. It's important for everyone to be the little guy from time to time. It builds character, he says, it builds empathy. It puts in perspective all the things that we take for granted. I realize now that I had never been to a place where I didn't speak the language.

I tell him I had just found out I'm brown the other day in English class. He laughs asking how so. I tell him that my English teacher is an older hippie and the semester revolved around the Sixties and we were discussing Civil Rights. I've always been a fan of that era and have probably read more about the conflict between Malcolm X and Martin Luther King Jr. than anyone else in the class so I was always the one arguing and rebutting. At the end of one of the classes, I approached her and apologized for speaking on behalf of people of color and that I recognized it was not my place to talk on their experiences when we had so little in common. She said it actually was my place and if anyone else said anything then it wouldn't have had as big an impact. It was just then that I realized I was brown. I always knew I was an Arab Muslim, but it never occurred to me that I was... brown. Not just that, but I was the token brown kid. He laughs again and says sometimes realizing who you are doesn't come from contemplation in the mirror, but a small comment or incident no one saw coming.

I've driven on this highway so many times I know the hills and turns and tollbooths like the back of my hand. I chose to reserve a shuttle as opposed to taking a Mega Bus because I need reliability today despite how much more it costs. I remember buying a ticket from Christiansburg,

Virginia to Washington, DC one time when I went to Virginia Tech a couple of years ago. Needless to say, the trip did not really go as planned. We stood out in the freezing cold for an hour past the departure time. As people began getting testy, a lady passenger, who was a reporter by trade, called the Mega Bus HQ to ask about the status of the bus and they reassuringly told her it'll be there soon. She called again about an hour after that, and it was a different, more honest operator. The lady startled all the passengers by suddenly yelling into the phone that her next story was going to be about how her lawyer boyfriend tore Mega Bus a new one for this disaster! As it turned out, our bus had left forty minutes before the departure time and they'd just then sent us another bus from DC to arrive within the next four hours. I ended up hitching a ride with two other Virginia Tech students with this one petite white girl who was instead driving her grandmother's little car up in spite of the mess. All I could think about was how she ended up driving Al-Qaida in the form of Abdul from Saudi, Ali from Iran, and Mohammad from India as long as we all split the cost of the tank of gas. I never read anything about the online or in any newspapers, I do however still hope that lady kept true to her word and sued them for all they were worth. That wasn't the only time I got shafted by Mega Bus, nor was it the last, but when it's the only mode of transport out of Blacksburg, then I took it however many times I needed to. I digress, today I can't afford to take the risk; the weather isn't in my favor, and I have too long a trip to start it off wrong.

We keep talking. He tells me he used to be a bus driver down south and gives me tips on how to deal with the shitty ones. He tells me a bunch of unwritten rules and rituals bus and truck drivers all over the country have, and how his time in Spain allowed him limited entry into the Hispanic community since he was different, knows what it's like to be a foreigner, and also sort of spoke the language. It's been a fun couple of hours, but eventually we have to end it as we arrive at Chicago O'Hare. He doesn't allow me to tip him since I'm likely going to need the spare change throughout the trip, tells me to tip him when I got back from vacation. I like him, he is cool.

Deux

Checking in my duffle bag and going through security is a lot easier and quicker than I expected. Since 9/11, traveling has become much more difficult than it used to be for me as a kid and this is the first time I've ever not been "randomly selected." I'm hoping the rest of the trip goes this well. I wish all my trips were like this.

There still is about an hour before we start boarding. I pull out my camera and take a few pictures. There is something so charming about international airports. However hectic and sometimes frustrating as the experience may be, it's still a little remarkable to see people preparing to use the scientific feat of manned flight to somewhere they've never been. Soldiers going to or coming back from war, a family reuniting for the first time in months or even years, or just people in suits simply going about their business. Even the staff employed here dress differently than they would if they worked in an office building or mall or workshop. Airports are such a break from the humdrum of life in the city as they are all different but similar enough, and sometimes almost feel like a series of connected cities within their walls.

I see a man and his daughter and ask them if they mind being the subject of a couple pictures. I just really liked how he stood holding her, looking out the window at the airplanes and ground crew as he explains to her simple functions and how things work. Louis CK once said in an interview that parents are like tour guides for their children and it's up to them to make the world a worthy place to witness. I see a heavy machine operator who looks like Clint Eastwood and take a photo of him. He doesn't look like he's enjoying his time, but who would working for American Airlines, let alone suffer the Windy City's December weather.

I should land in Paris in about nine hours and I hope my two and a half hour layover there is long enough for me to find my next plane to Jeddah. I've only ever been to Paris once before. My mother, sisters, and my seven year old self were flying home from DC and we had a seven hour layover. Even then they wouldn't allow us one day visas so we were stuck in the airport the whole time. I was very young and don't recall much more than snapshots, but Charles De Gaulle was a large airport and I hope I don't get lost finding my gate.

A woman's voice comes on the PA system and announces that our plane is under emergency maintenance and there will be some delays. A control surface on one of the plane's wings is malfunctioning and the mechanics are working as fast as they can to fix it. It'll only be a little while before we board. Knowing American Airlines, these delays are routine procedures, and at worst they'll redirect my flight if I happen to miss it in Paris. I keep telling myself everything has been perfect so far, I won't allow this little hiccup to ruin my excitement. I'm already ahead of schedule anyway.

Having found one of those new charging stations, I take my laptop out of my bag and open up my photography folder and reminisce over the past few years I've been here. I've been to so many places and have met so many people. It's a little sad considering that you could be best friends with someone and as soon as your tenure in the place you're at ends, so too does all contact you have with the person. You can fight it all you want, and I have, but it always goes the same way. I suppose that even though communication has advanced as far as being able to know exactly how drunk someone got on their birthday even if they're on the other side of the world, in reality, unless you were there, it still doesn't really matter.

Everybody goes about their days the same, as if all the people around them are just part of an interactive background which we all knowingly or unknowingly participate in nonetheless. It's almost sociopathic to think, but what if everyone is in fact just a figment of my imagination, a part of the Matrix, a robot, an actor like in The Truman Show, or just a cardboard shell with a voice that only affects my psyche? These thoughts, I reckon, occur to everyone and I'm no different. Maybe it's just a defense mechanism to justify or rationalize the hurt one goes through when others move on.

I catch myself before I get too overwhelmed with thought and open the folder to see what lies within: California; Colorado; DC; Kansas; Illinois; Indiana; Iowa; Maryland; Massachusetts; New York; Pennsylvania; Tennessee; Wisconsin; Virginia. I have traveled quite a lot. So many stories to tell, I can't wait to be home so I could share them.

Trois

Lana Del Rey's *"Born To Die"* starts playing from my phone. It almost commands a tear as I listen and relate to the concept that the destiny of some people is not to live long and have children and stability but rather to explode with life at an early age, like the death of a young star turning into a supernova the ripples of which are dangerous and beautiful. Life isn't about how long you survive, but what it is you survive.

It's easy to be afraid when you have so much to lose. People spend their whole lives accumulating stuff-whether it's money and material objects, certificates of authority and recognition, friends and kin, or even the healthy ones look to have the longest lives. Everybody has somewhere to go and something to do with or for someone else. Not many people just sit and do nothing and appreciate existence.

My roommate, Wiz, taught me this. I used to get so frustrated when I'd ask him what he's doing later and he'd say "Nothing." I'd then ask him if he'd like to join me in an activity, he'd decline saying he had plans already. I ask him to explain then, how does he have plans and yet is free later. He'd say, "I did not say I wasn't doing anything, I said I'm doing Nothing." Meaning his planned activity will be to sit down and exist. It was quite the realization to me; that sometimes existing is enough a thing to do. We don't always have to sedate ourselves from the emptiness of existence, sometimes to stare it in the face and call it beautiful is sufficient for a good time.

"Born to Die" is like that. Lana here discusses that life isn't about the mainstream idea of success and business, but rather to explore what Robert Frost would call *"The Road Not Taken."* And if we die on that road, then it will be beautiful.

Wiz has taught me many other things. We met in Riyadh in 2011 on our way to Virginia. The other guys on the program and I had either been to the US many times or were Americans themselves. This was Wiz's first venture outside of Saudi, which he has only seen very little of to begin with. He was what we would call a "FOB" or "fresh off the boat." This meant that he had very little exposure to the outside world, was very prone to culture shock, and that his mannerisms were likely to be much more appropriate at home. At that time, I had a sincere and utter disgust for the people of my country. The way they spoke and acted and conducted themselves around places of knowledge and culture was very unlike my ideals. Wiz coming from a small town in the middle of nowhere was not a good sign.

Somewhere down the line at Tech, things became clear and the cliché "Never judge a book by its cover" had never made more sense. Of all the people in our group, Wiz was by far the coolest. He was smart, albeit not very ambitious, grateful, hilarious, loyal, and kind. Everyone wanted to be his friend. Everyone trusted him. He is worth every ounce of love he's ever gotten and then some.

We were actually in Baltimore, Maryland the day the first part of our program ended. A handful of us at Tech attended a summer semester at Johns Hopkins as a requisite before beginning our undergraduate careers, which would be the second part. By this time Wiz and I and the others had gotten exceptionally close. I remember briefly waving to them as my cab came to take me to the airport to fly away. After all that time together, getting to know each other, working, playing, loving, laughing, fighting, and forgetting, it was time for us to go our separate paths. I didn't want to show it, but as I got in the elevator with my suitcase after our goodbyes, I started crying inconsolably. It felt as though a part of me died and the next step won't be nearly as monumental. It was the sad ending to a beautiful story of adventure, rebellion, and kinship.

What I hadn't realized in that moment was that Wiz and I were attending the same school in Madison, Wisconsin, next semester and that we'd even be living together. It actually didn't really hit me until I saw him in Madison a few hours after I'd landed. By then, however, we were different people, no longer rookie freshmen, no longer fresh off the boat. I had just recently broken up with Lamees for the first time relating to some things that may or may not have happened in Virginia; and he had become "close friends" with his crush. Furthermore, another student from our program who we had met at Hopkins was joining us that year and the three of us had the same English class. We were a force to be reckoned with, but it wasn't the same as it was anymore, and it wasn't as beautiful.

As I listen to "Born To Die," I realize now that it may also be applied to moments as well as people. Mortality isn't necessary for death in a relative sense. Sometimes somebody you know dies without having to stop breathing or losing their job even, but by no longer sharing their experience of life with you and thus no longer existing to you as more than a ghost in pictures haunting you through a screen in your palm like a Ouija board. Looking back at it now, as the song comes to an end, some experiences were born to die, and that's absolutely fine.

Quatre

Lamees and I had gotten back together after that semester, but by then my scholarship had sent me to Kansas to join a group they had there, similar to mine in Virginia. I had bought a car in Madison but I my advisor wouldn't let me drive it down and had booked me a flight instead, saying she was afraid I'd be late. I still found a way to miss the flight and catch the next one down.

I was to live in an apartment with two guys I'd never met before in my life. They were Chinese and I refused to hold any preconceptions. I don't recall ever being friends with any Chinese people before. I've been friends with Koreans, Filipinos, and some Japanese. I understood racist stereotypes and how they don't mean much in the real world. I wasn't going to let any "Asian" jokes get in the way of a wonderful opportunity to expand my cultural expedition in the US.

As I walked in the door, I introduced myself and shook hands with them and we talked for a little bit. One of the guys wasn't home; he never really was, I don't recall ever even meeting him. The other had his girlfriend living with us and I was borderline jealous I could never have that experience. The girl's name was Xiao, the word meaning Smile in Mandarin, the boy introduced himself as John and he was Cantonese, together they were the Chens. Their wifi was "Chen Family," I thought it was cute.

They celebrated their lunar new year during my first week there and invited me to join them for dinner before they went dancing. I thought of it as a nice gesture and dressed up. I always knew that the Chinese food we know and love did not represent what the Chinese actually ate and I was excited to taste what they and their friends had made, traditional recipes from across China, and it smelled intriguing. It was also that day that cemented in my mind never to experiment with food I didn't understand again. Though they enjoyed it with splendor and a sense of nostalgia that I truly understand eating rice and meat like I did with my grandfather before he died, the mix of textures and flavors that I had tried that day did not sit well with me. All I remember was peanut butter tasting chicken that was chewy like taffy in a soup they kept replenishing with ingredients laid out on the table. I didn't go dancing with them, I understood that I wasn't that close quite yet.

As the semester went on, I tried to show interest in them. They didn't speak English very well, but enough for us to communicate. Xiao was studying journalism and John was studying accounting. They met in a math class they took in their first year, and they were juniors when I stumbled in. We had a couple of conversations about the differences in culture within China, the struggles of Taiwan and the South China Sea, life in America as foreigners and the value of education. They told me the Arabic language was a highly sought after skill where they were from, and teaching it there could do me well. I tried teaching them the alphabets and how Western Mathematics can trace its roots to a medieval Muslim philosopher. I'm better at math than I am at Arabic, but I don't think either topic really captivated them.

It became clear to me not much later that they really weren't as invested in this exchange as I was and were actually annoyed by my presence. They always seemed to have a friend over, either to study or just to hang out, and sometimes they were drunk and passed out around the house making it a little uncomfortable for me to move about. It was like we were in the wild and they had marked their territory and I intruded and was not welcome. I stayed in my room most of the time I was there, otherwise I'd try to stay on campus as much as possible.

The guys in the program weren't much of a family like we were in Virginia. They were also mainly FOBs and were probably afraid of me because they didn't know why I was there, thinking I may be a spy from the program. In reality, I barely knew why I was there.

Once the semester ended, I was glad to see everyone go. I had to stay a few more weeks as my lease only ended in August. The Chens took their wifi with them and all I was left with was my laptop and some movies on a hard drive, but even that broke one night and I lost all the photographs and film and research I had gathered over the past few years. It was a sad and lonely period in my life. I was diagnosed with Major Depressive Disorder.

My mother and younger sister visited the US that summer and I went to join them in DC and NYC. It was an excellent and well needed change in scenery and I couldn't be more happy to join them. We spent a week in each city and road tripped from one to the other stopping by Baltimore so I could see Hopkins one last time. Like making eye contact for an instant with the love who got away, that night in Baltimore was full of emotion and internal conflict.

The next couple of tracks to play on my phone are Brooklyn and Baltimore's Fireflies by Woodkid. I feel every word as it flows through me like my blood in a shiver.

Cinq

I flew back to Wisconsin for spring break that semester and Wiz and I drove the truck from there to visit a friend we had met at Hopkins in Knoxville, Tennessee then back to Kansas. Wiz met the Chens and probably had a better relationship with them than I had. He flew back at the end of the week. It may have been the highlight of my time in Kansas until leaving it.

Most of the time the truck was with me it needed some fixing. The man I bought it from didn't seem to take care of it very well. He was a car salesman and sold it to me as his personal vehicle but through his dealership so I naïvely trusted him. It was the first vehicle I had ever purchased myself and I ended up spending more than three times what I bought it for in maintenance and repairs, but it was worth every cent.

I made it a habit to take a two thousand mile drive with the truck at least once a year. She presented herself with the name Alexander The

Great, the conqueror of all. Though cars and trucks are often referred to with feminine pronouns and names, she had the persona of a historical, ultra masculine homosexual, the name made sense to me and all who knew her.

My next road trip was leaving Kansas. I had explained to my friends all over the US that I am leaving and will likely never be in the next state over to Colorado again in my life, and that I plan to drive by there before going back to Wisconsin.

The scholarship and I decided after the semester to go our separate ways since their micromanaging of my life was not something I was willing to submit to, and it would be quite a waste of resources for them to try to change that. So it was settled; I was going back to Wisco, but not back to the University. I was now free.

Of all the people I tried to contact, the one person I disliked the most in Madison was the only person who flew down to help me move back and drive to CO. His name's Faisal and he was in Madison on a different program than that Wiz and I were on. I don't know what made him do it, I'm sure he was as reluctant about it as I was, but he accepted the invitation and I welcomed the company.

Faisal and I went to a hookah bar the night he arrived in Lawrence. There we met the proprietors of traditional Arabic smoking pipe tobacco that I have been buying from for as long as I've been in the US. The man running the bar was Lebanese and has hooked us up with some pipe cleaning supplies and samples of different tobacco blends. He also told us of the medical marijuana dispensary he goes to in Denver that often doesn't ask for prescriptions or even ID. We thought to make that our destination. We left Lawrence the next day.

On our way to Colorado, I made it a point to stop by Topeka, the home of the Westboro Baptist Church. We even intended to get baptized there as a joke, but to our luck, nobody was home. We did, however, meet their neighbors, an LGBT+ activist group who had purchased the house across from the WBC and painted it in a rainbow pattern to prove a point. The kind young man who opened the door spoke to us for a couple of minutes about what they do, what they represent, and how living so close to the most hated family in America and their political worst enemies was. To our hubristic surprise, the WBC turned out to be decent, civil neighbors when the cameras were off. We told him about the grim situation of heteronormivity in Saudi and how it's even more difficult to experiment and express yourself there than it is in the most conservative parts of the US. Once he saw my camera, he pointed at some signs on the yard saying that the house was open to having its picture taken, and even encouraged it. Faisal was wearing a Pink Floyd shirt, and the morning light was perfect. I took one of the greatest pictures in my life, and I still hold it dear.

We listened to a lot of Hip-Hop on the trip. I used to spend hours upon hours listening to early Rap and Rn'B in high school, dissecting rhyme patterns, flows, themes, content, and beats. Faisal wasn't as taken with Crooklyn Cuts as I was, he was more into Black Sabbath. I respected that immensely, but the screaming was difficult for me to understand so I made him read me the lyrics while I drove and we discussed the philosophical content with great fervor and interest.

My respect for Faisal grew by the minute and I regretted not giving him much of a chance while in Madison the first time. He then asked me if I listened to Pink Floyd, whose shirt he was wearing. I told him I only knew The Wall because of my father, and besides, who didn't want teachers to leave them alone in school growing up? He asked me if I had ever listened to Dark Side of The Moon. I told him I've heard of it, but was never interested enough to check it out. He told me to just shut up and listen as he played it. We drove past the Kansas border into Colorful Colorado and the terrain changed to accommodate the mood.

I can say with all honesty that my life can be split into two periods, pre and post Dark Side of The Moon. I was a new person at the end of the album. Baptized in the holy water of music, pain, understanding, fate and circumstance. Never have I been so moved by anything so clearly. I had read the Quran, the Bible, the Bhagavad Gita, the Tao, and many other religious and philosophical texts before, I had been to the top of the London Eye and to the pyramids in Giza, but none had done to me what that album did. And for that, I thank Faisal.

We arrived in Denver sixteen hours after leaving Lawrence and stopped at the place the barkeep told us about. As we parked and prepared our cash, a man stepped out of the passenger side of the car next to us going in to resupply himself. I asked if they required a prescription, and he said they did. He offered to buy us some if we would agree to drive him to his next destination. We handed him the money hoping he wouldn't rip us off, but he stayed true and so did we.

He had gotten us half an ounce worth of a variety of his favorite strands, and another half in edibles. He also gave us his number to give to anyone we knew visiting Denver in the near future. I saved it on my phone. His name was Daniel, and I still have his number.

Paranoid about traveling through Nebraska, Iowa, and about a hundred miles into Wisconsin with what we had, we went to the nearest 711 and bought a bunch of snacks that matched the edibles and Faisal repackaged everything to be as inconspicuous as possible. We even bought a large Monster Energy Drink can with the tin cap to hide the bud in and tossed it into our garbage bag alongside a bunch of other consumed Red Bulls, Monsters and candy wraps.

Faisal has poor eyesight at night and once the caffeine began wearing off we stopped to spend the night at a roadside motel in Fort Morgan, Colorado, almost halfway between Denver and the state border. It was a clear and quiet night except for trucks on the highway, the sky was vast and the stars struck me for the first time. I had always appreciated astronomy, but never have I really seen the sky this way. Maybe Dark Side of The Moon was presenting itself to me in a way I never expected, or maybe it was the euphoria of leaving my life in Kansas behind.

During the last few weeks in Kansas before the Chens left, I used to occupy my time learning about astrophysics and the universe. I must have watched every one of Neil deGrasse Tyson's lectures available for free on the internet and was able to bootleg Carl Sagan's Cosmos series. I learned so much about the sky, but I had never observed it in all its glory until that night with Faisal. It may have also been the weed.

We got to Madison the next day's afternoon. I called Wiz to gather the guys for a cookout. It was the beginning of the rest of my life, and I was ready.

Six

I notice a man walk up to the lady at the desk by the gate and remove my headphones to listen for updates. She comes on the PA system again and tells us that the plane is still not ready and won't be for at least another hour. There is a loud, almost synchronized sigh from the passengers like we all unanimously agree that this is bullshit but there isn't anything we can do about it. We're already half an hour late. I pack my things for the time being, go up to the lady and ask her if she's sure it'll be at least an hour and if I have time to wander around the airport instead of just waiting in anguish and anxiety. She looks at me with the kind eyes of someone who is relieved by my nonaggressive tone and appreciates my adventurous curiosity. She tells me there's plenty of time and that she'll page the general airport PA if the plane is ready beforehand. I thank her and make my way through the displeased crowd.

There are very few airports in the world I

didn't enjoy being in. I always try to dissociate the traveling and the delays and everything from the airports themselves. I wonder what the Wright Brothers would think if they were to see O'Hare; or what Darwin would think seeing people drop the façade of civility and revert to their natural instincts. As far as we've come as a species, once we're traveling, it all goes away. People are much more open to displaying how they truly feel. They communicate without using words like the groan from earlier, and when they do use words, a lot of the time it's in anger. Queues are forced and nobody is considerate of order, let alone anyone else. People sleeping on the ground gripping their luggage with their whole lives as if there are threats of being mugged regardless of all the security officers and cameras. Swathes of people dispersed all around, each looking for their food and shelter. Mothers keeping their young close to them but are too tired to be playful and caring. Fathers circling the herd making sure no predators come close. "If you see something, say something." Each probably hoping to be the hero who stops the next terrorist attack while simultaneously hoping it never comes to that. I feel my movements being followed by threatened gazes, but fear not, I'm not doing anything wrong.

I think about the airports I've been to in the US and what they've meant to me. I started smoking cigarettes after a year and a half of being clean in an airport in Atlanta. I heard French in an Indian accent at JFK in New York. I fell in love with the art all around Baltimore International. Before Saudi Airlines flew directly to DC in the 1990s, I flew in a prop plane for the first time with my father from LaGuardia to Reagan where the height of the ceiling and the symmetry of the arches always leave me in awe. The Kansas City airport was very dreary and depressing, but the one in Madison was very clean and classy.

I see a Five Guys and decide to have a burger made by this lovely lady who asks about my camera. I take a portrait of her and show her the quality of the image. I eat and tip her well. She had a beautiful smile and I want so badly to enjoy this hour I have before leaving.

When I was in Virginia, almost any flight I took to or from Roanoke Regional had to pass by Charlotte, North Carolina, since it was the closest airport big enough to fly more than a couple hundred miles. In reality, the Charlotte airport was huge. It took more than half an hour to walk from the terminal servicing small planes to where the larger jets were and there wasn't any express railway like in O'Hare, Dulles, and other large airports- at least none I knew about.

The scholarship once hosted an emergency meeting for all its students in the US at Georgia Tech when I was in VT, so the group Wiz and I were a part of had to fly to Atlanta through Charlotte late at night before the meeting took place. We were to be there for just one night. It was during exam week so we were already very stressed and tired, and there wasn't any other way to get there as everything was very last minute.

We had a bit of a layover but it was our first time at that airport so we rushed to find our gate and agreed that if we had any time to spare we would all get our own food and meet back to study for our calculus test we had postponed to Wednesday from Tuesday, when it was scheduled to be and will be for the other classes taking it with the same professor.

One of my roommates and I were delighted to find a Bojangles' at our terminal and decided to eat from there. Bojangles' is a southern style fried chicken joint, similar to KFC but less commercial and it felt and tasted cleaner. It's very close to and tasted a lot like Al Baik in Jeddah, which at this point I can't wait to get home and have.

This roommate and I had a memory together

discovering Bojangles' in VT before the night in Charlotte. Around our second or third week there, one of the girls in the program had forgotten her phone on a bus one night coming home from class, and the next day called the station asking if they had found a Black Berry Torch on the HWD A route bus from midnight. The operator said they had, but, ironically, there were no bus routes that stop at the station. The operator did, however tell the girl where the nearest stop was and that the station was a short walk from there. Two of my roommates and I offered to accompany her on the trek to find the phone. I had a tablet with GPS that could help direct us, and my roommates didn't feel comfortable letting me go alone with her since they could sense us being infatuated with one another, and they were right to some degree to suspect that.

We got off at the bus stop at around 11.00am but only got to the station at 2.00. It was a much longer walk than the operator implied it would be. Maybe she expected us to know the short cuts, be on bikes, or at the very least be more fit. We got the phone and started walking back to the bus stop, and got hungry along the way and found a gas station with a Bojangles'. We had never tried it before and didn't know what to expect, so we decided to give it a shot and immediately fell in love with it. After learning how taxis worked in Blacksburg, we returned to the place a number of times throughout the year. The smell of the chicken that night at the airport was like a breath of fresh air.

The things you can buy at airports are pretty ridiculous especially considering what isn't allowed to go through security. The TSA make such a fuss over a bottle of water when you can still get shitfaced drunk just past the checkpoint or even in most airplanes. Some airports sell cigarettes and have smoking rooms but won't sell lighters. Everything is so much more expensive at the Duty Frees than it would be at the gas station's mini market just down the street from the airport. O'Hare was no different, so I buy some super expensive Nyquil pills to help me sleep during the flight and keep exploring with my camera in hand and backpack on, checking the time regularly.

There is a small fighter plane on exhibit in a corner between two terminals. The plaque says it belonged to Captain O'Hare himself, the namesake of the airport. He used to be a navy pilot in the second world war. It figures that most of our technological achievements as a species were either for impressing our mates, worshipping someone or something, or killing each other. Sex, drugs, and rock n' roll.

It's getting pretty late into the hour and I still haven't heard any news from the PA about my plane and the screens showing flight details still say mine is delayed. I stop by an electronics kiosk and buy some meaningless gifts for family before I start heading back to the gate. It looks like my luck from earlier is beginning to wear off.

Sept

The gate opens about a half hour after I got back. My two and a half hours in Paris have diminished and an American Airlines operator tells us that we will have redirected flights ready once we land in Paris and apologizes for the inconvenience. I find my seat by a window, stow away my backpack under the seat in front of me, and keep my camera in hand for takeoff and cloud pictures. Not long after the seatbelt light is turned off, the Nyquil begins to kick in and I lean my seat back and go to sleep. It's a seven hour flight, I hope things go well in Paris.

Huit

The first thing I do as I get off the plane is check the information screen at the end of the jet way to see what the status of my flight is. I'm supposed to take the daily flight from Paris to Jeddah on Saudia, and I see that it is currently departing. There's no possible way I could catch it or have it wait.

As promised, the lady at the American Airlines desk in the terminal hands me a new itinerary that lands me in Jeddah twenty minutes before midnight and it's 1.00pm already. Today is Christmas Eve. I wish her a merry Christmas and get on my way.

My next flights are on Lufthansa from Paris to Frankfurt where I have two more hours of layover then on Saudia back to Jeddah. I've been to the Frankfurt airport before. It feels more like a mechanism than an organism almost like a German stereotype, but what I am really looking forward to are the Camel themed smoking lounges; I could use a cigarette at this point, or five. I have a high school friend near Frankfurt, he told me once that if I'm ever even at the airport to call him and he'd pass by. I don't think I want to risk missing the flight from there to Jeddah because of seeing him. He's going to Jeddah too this week, I'll just see him there.

For spring break in Virginia, most of the gang went down to Miami but I chose to visit a buddy of mine in Boston. Siraj and I were very good friends in high school and I used to tutor him and a couple of other guys. We all graduated a semester early. He moved to Boston to study business hoping to take after his father. I spent the week with him, teaching him how to make basic breakfast and his laundry and other such things people in Jeddah often take for granted. We decided to have one last cigarette before I got on the plane to fly back to Virginia and those two minutes cost me the flight. I'd hate to repeat that mistake in Germany.

My next flight leaves in an hour and a half so I get moving toward my new gate. I'll explore the airport another time. I've been here before and I'm sure I'll be back here again soon enough. Since the flight is within the European Union, then it's considered domestic. I leave the international terminal and try to pass immigration security to get to the other terminal.

There are two young ladies in uniform and the dark haired one asks for my passport. She flips through it a couple of times and asks her colleague something in French, I don't understand it. They both look concerned and look at me as if I am somebody.

The officer asks me where I'm going in broken English and I tell her Jeddah through Frankfurt. She asks me for a Schengen visa, which I don't have so I ask if there's something wrong. She explains to me that it's illegal for me to fly within Europe without one. I ask her how that can be if airports are considered international territory and I wouldn't be leaving the airport. She says it's about the security on domestic flights being different than around international terminals and I cannot pass through her check point.

I had just gotten off a long flight from the United States that was delayed and now I have to travel an additional 5 hours through another country to go home. I don't want to hear her tell me there's something wrong. I tell her there must be a mistake, if I could go back to the American Airlines desk, I can have the trip rerouted again and not go through this nonsense. I just want to go home already. She looks slightly empathetic but shakes her head "Non."

She takes me to an Air France desk and argues with the man there and he looks at me like he can do nothing. Anxiety starts pouring into my chest and I begin to get nervous and angry. I ask the officer again if we can go to the American Airlines desk and have this figured out. This is partly because I'd like to understand why she seems so concerned, but again she denies the notion, and says the words "Police Station." There definitely is something wrong.

Neuf

The officer takes me across the terminal past some restricted entry doors and up a flight of stairs. The whole building is concrete covered in aluminum and stainless steel. It's intimidatingly modern and brutal. It is confusing, cold, and for a second, even sinister.

The hallway is rather narrow and dark but as we approach the constable's office it gets brighter, warmer, and louder. I hear a fat old man yelling on the phone and boots running out of sync and in different directions. The officer has grown some compassion for me probably sensing my fear and gives me a reassuring nod and a smile.

At the end of the hall before the office there are some typical airport bench seats she tells me to sit on and wait. She walks into the office with the yelling holding my passport and itinerary. The yelling stops and I only hear a murmur of what I wouldn't understand anyway. I wait for what feels like forever before she opens the door and walks toward me. She tells me everything is going to be alright and she'll check up on me again at the end of her shift if I'm not out by then. I don't know whether to be relieved, grateful, or frightened by her promise.

I stand and look toward the office but the man at the desk motions for me to sit back down. He was fat and bald and red from all the earlier yelling. I sit down and notice that right in front of me is a room with men in their late twenties laughing, loosely dressed in uniform and a stainless steel table and an empty chair. It was an interrogation room. I didn't do anything wrong.

A black officer walks out of the interrogation room and offers me candy. I notice that it's rum chocolate and refuse one. The Quran directly bans the consumption of alcohol, not that I should be any tipsy or even slightly buzzed not knowing what's going on or where I'm going next. He shrugs and goes on his way back toward the airport. The laughing quiets down and I don't hear any yelling from the office.

The quiet calms my fear temporarily but heightens my anxiety. I think back to all the steps I've taken to get here and what I could've done to bother the European Union before then. I understand that this is probably typical protocol for visa issues, but what else could they find about and hold over me?

I reach for my phone and one of the men inside the room in front of me leaps over and grabs it. He tells me to carry my backpack onto the table and open it so they can search through what I have in there. Only some electronics and a toothbrush. They tell me to take off my shoes, sweater as well and pat me down presumably looking for weapons or drugs.

The question I learned to ask from awareness programs as well my own altercations with the law in the US was if I was free. Unfortunately the officers don't seem to understand what I'm asking. I realize that for the first time in my life, I don't speak the language. I felt absolutely trapped and hopeless. They take my phone, camera, laptop, tablet, and the wireless keyboard I got my dad from Chicago and tell me to go sit down again. I am naked in spite of my clothes and completely unknown, trapped and hopeless. I still did nothing wrong.

Dix

Moments or hours later the office door opens and the fat man tells me to come in. I walk into the smoke filled room and ask if I could smoke but was denied. The man asks me what my name and date of birth are to confirm the papers in his hand. He then asks me if I knew why I'm in here. I tell him it's likely my supposed flight to Germany, which has left by now. He is not amused by the matter-of-fact attitude that even I didn't know I had in me. He stands up and walks me to the interrogation room and have the men there check me and my stuff again under his supervision. This time one of them was writing down the contents of my bag. They took everything from me but my clothes and the chain I'm wearing that says "Never Never Never Give up."

I ordered this overpriced pendant for Lamees from a Duty Free magazine on the flight from Virginia to Boston and completely forgot about it. I got a phone call several months later when I was in Baltimore that the sales department had just received the order and asked if I still wanted it, and I said yes. I had them deliver it to the friend who lived in Tennessee throughout the year since I still didn't have an address by then. Wiz and I drove to get it on the way to Kansas but she had lost it during her move back home, only to find it and mail it to another friend, Joe, at MIT who I drove from Wisconsin a year later to see to get the necklace. I will deliver it.

The fat man says something and walks back to his office. I try to follow him but the guards stop me and take me to a backroom they have a window overlooking. It's very bright colored with blinding lights. It's the main source of light in the interrogation room, which is hidden behind a mirror window from this side. It's the shape of the inside of a quarter of an oval with a concrete bench stretching alongside the concave end. A chill crawls up my spine as they close the door behind me which can only be opened from their side.

I wonder if knowing French would've helped me at all or if I weren't an Arab. Is this how the Cubans felt landing in Florida in the 80s or how African and Desi people feel going to Saudi? Why is this face of France never shown, or ours for that matter? Is this normal practice or am I a special case, and if so is that good or bad? I catch myself pacing the room in worry and thought like if I were to ignore turning around then the distance I could walk would be toward freedom. I don't know how long it's been since I came here.

The door opens and I immediately snap back and instinctively walk toward it. It's just a social worker offering me a slice of baguette, some tuna, chips, and a sealed plastic cup of water. Thanks. A little after that, an African man is brought in, says his Salaams, lies down on the concrete bench like he's been here before, and immediately falls into deep sleep. The food satisfied one of my hungers but I still need to know what's happening and can't relax until I do. I envy my cellmate.

Realizing it would be awhile, I sit down and start looking around the room. It is about thirty feet long and maybe fifteen feet deep. The paint on the concrete wall extends down over the curved bench built onto it. The top half is white, the lower half is painted a sort of creamy yellow with black marks like shoe prints scratched across the bottom. The lights were bright florescent and they were in six sets of four. There are no ceiling tiles and you could see the air ducts and wiring harnesses and plumbing. The door was simple wooden with a small barred window, the handle on this side is removed.

A guard comes in and gives the African man his baguette and chips and water and calls for me to go to the office again. I hope this is finally over. I still don't know what I did wrong to get here.

The fat man brought in a translator who looks and sounds very drunk celebrating the night. He spoke worse English than the fat man but they hand me a number which I put in my pocket, and tell me I'll be going to a hotel for the night. The fat man calls an officer from the interrogation room to have me checked one last time and to be handed just my phone to contact family until further notice.

It's a BlackBerry and only has my American SIM card, I never had a stable number in Saudi, I must have changed it a dozen times by the time I left to Virginia. I call my parents and tell them that I'm stuck in a police holding room in Paris and not to worry, I should be home soon.

I call Lamees telling her the plan is off since I don't really know when I'll even be back at this point. I tell her I love her and that I'll do whatever I can to see her before I have to go back to the US. I tell her I have something to give her and I will deliver it.

The officers lock me back up with the sleeping African man who has eaten his food and left his rubbish on the floor because there's no garbage bin in the room. I still have my phone but I can't take pictures knowing they're looking at me. So I sit in silence between poor quality calls with my parents who are freaking out and a heartbroken girlfriend. I decide to turn the phone off and keep it with them. I'm already afraid and they aren't helping. I check the time before giving away the phone. It's 7.20pm. I've been here for almost six hours.

Onze

I try to follow my cellmate's lead and put my hoodie up, lie down and go to sleep. Then I remember the funniest thing. The scholarship offered to sponsor the students in my cohort to go to a weeklong event that fits in with their major, like a seminar or a science fair, during the summer.

Before going to Baltimore, Joe and I decided we'd test and see how far the program would send us. We took our chances and asked to go to the Netherlands quoting that the contract did not limit the events to within any country. They immediately rejected without even allowing us to explain why we chose that event in particular. But having the bar set so high, we then bargained our way down to a seminar in computation in high energy plasma held at the Institute for Pure and Applied Mathematics in UCLA.

Joe was an International Physics Olympics winner and a high school friend and I did some work in computation in super low energy condensate, so we both felt confident that we could hold our own at this sort of seminar. We didn't lose sight of why we were really going there, though. After all, Joe did introduce me to smoking up.

So I made the call to Los Angeles asking how to register and the man told me it's a post-graduates seminar with some of the highest ranking physicists in the country and asked me what our qualifications were. I told him who we were and about the scholarship who would be funding it and that Joe and I were both attending Virginia Tech and were transferring to even higher ranking schools in the fall. He didn't seem convinced but sighed and agreed to email me the link to the private registration site.

The next Sunday morning, Joe and I smoked, hopped on a series of planes across the country and landed at LAX in the afternoon. We took a cab to the hotel the scholarship booked for us. The drive was pleasant and the sun was warm and the palm trees were as high as they are in the movies. The streets were wide and crowded and the city was colorful. It was a good change of atmosphere from Virginia's rural Appalachian vibe.

It was a five star hotel essentially on campus with large jugs of fruit infused ice cold water

49

and coffee in the lobby. All the major surfaces were dark marble and polished granite. People were dressed in nice suits and dresses. Everyone was very rich and white, and there we were, him in swimming trunks and me in my favorite cargo shorts. Joe and I liked it.

We went upstairs to check out the room we shared. It was on the twelfth floor with two single beds. The wifi worked and Joe put all his clothes in the closet and got extra comfy. I was hungry and was looking for where IPAM was for the next day and where food was within walking distance for the night.

IPAM was a twenty minute walk away, there didn't seem to be any bus routes that would make that time shorter and the cab fare from the airport was expensive. Joe calls our coordinator and asks if they'll pay for us to rent a car. They obviously refuse again, but offer to pay the cab fare from and to the airport if we sent the receipts. It was worth a shot.

We shut the laptop off and went down to check out the campus while there was still light. We found the typical arrangement of fast food and clothing stores, nothing really worth mentioning. We did however spot a medicinal dispensary and were intrigued to find out if there was any way for us to buy from there. The pharmacist was very threatening and angry that I'd dare ask. He said only if I had a medical card and I can only get that if I lived in CA. Joe and I left and it was getting dark so we walked a bit farther away from the hotel looking for real So Cal food. We found an In-n-Out Burger and had our dinner.

I've been to Los Angeles twice in my life. Once before I can remember and the second was exactly a year before then. A high school classmate and I had won a series of science fairs with our project and it ultimately ended at ISEF in LA in 2011, where we were finalists. This was what got me the opportunity to join this program with Wiz and Joe and them. It was a weeklong trip which was very hectic and exhausting and we were forced to enjoy ourselves and wear polo shirts that say "Saudi Team" on the back. I didn't like them then, but I wear them all the time now.

After dinner, Joe and I walked around the area until it was just past ten. We went back to the hotel and started googling transportation around us. I found a four year old forum post giving the first name and the street of a Middle Eastern rental car agent who hooked someone's cousin up and they weren't even 25 yet. After a little more research, I found the man's phone number. I gave it a call and in a heavy Turkish accent the man answered. He confirmed his name and asked me what I wanted. He sounded like he was somewhere crowded and was in a hurry. I told him Joe and I were both under 25 but would like to rent a car. He says he'd do it if we paid the heavy insurance premium and paid him up front for twice as long as we'd have it. He'll be available the next day at 1.30pm. Joe and I had been saving up for this trip, even though we didn't know it was to LA. We agreed to the terms and hung up.

Joe was already on a marijuana forum looking for less strict dispensaries and found a number of them on Venice Beach. I checked our plan for the seminar and saw a two hour lunch break starting at noon. We agreed to go get the car during the break, turned our lights off and went to sleep.

We got up at 6.00am the next morning hoping to catch the breakfast meet and greet at the seminar before registration started at 7.30. We showered and hiked our way to the place just as people were getting their coffees. We grabbed our food and starting walking around hoping to recognize some of the people. One of the professors judged our booth poorly at ISEF so I avoided contact with him. The coffee was alright, though.

Registration opened early and we received our programs, legal pads and some free pens, We also got lanyards with our names, fields of study, and the school we're attending. I had Virginia Tech, but Joe being a douche, told them he was going to MIT because that's where he'll be attending in the next year. It bit him in the ass though.

We sat down next to a skinny man working on some laminated device and some papers with code on them. Joe commented that it was a cool little waterproof calculator, and the man looked at Joe with the menacing look of the frustration of a million programmers trying to figure out how to calculate to what degree of sheer stupidity his observation was, and very plainly told Joe that it's an encrypter. The man told Joe he can't be from MIT since he knew all the faculty in the physics department and Joe tried to explain his blunder, but the man lost all interest after making his statement. This was not as good a start as we were expecting.

It was almost 8.00 and people started walking toward the large lecture hall. It was wide like it's usually split in two for separate purposes with a low wood beam ceiling. There was a large structural support pillar in the middle of the room between all the seats. Joe and I decided to sit there near the back. The lights were switched off but the sunlight coming from the windows above us lit the room in all its golden Californian glory. The people quieted down, the projector was turned on and the microphone was checked.

The professor I was avoiding earlier was the moderator throughout the week. He got up and introduced himself to the audience. He was very familiar with the crowd and even jokingly mocked a friend of his for being six years into his PhD and asked when will he finally finish and join the big boys. Joe and I were even more intimidated and anxious. We kept reminding ourselves this was what we signed up for, not just for the seminars, but as majors and careers. We also didn't forget about our rendezvous at 1.00pm.

The MC began introducing the premise of the seminar and quickly goes over some of what he considered the basics of the relevant quantum mechanics principles. The audience looked bored, he reassured them that he knows this is elementary, but pokes fun at the guy again calling him the late bloomer who might benefit from this for his homework. Several slides in, we realized that we've never seen some of these characters and symbols before and we both knew at least three languages to some degree of proficiency.

We then realized that the past three slides were all segments of the same equation and immediately confessed to ourselves and one another that this was way over our heads. We agreed that if we could each summarize everything we understood in half a legal pad page by the lunch break then we'd stay the whole week. When the break came, we couldn't combine our notes to make half a page and knew we weren't coming back.

Douze

The guards open the door and a man is shoved in with a loud groan and the door is slammed shut behind him. He tries to stop it but only ends up hurting his foot. He bangs the door yelling curses and insults in several languages. He paces the room and talks to himself like a mad man full of regret and concern. He catches me looking and starts talking to me in French. I tell him I speak English and Arabic, so he switches to Tunisian Arabic. I recognize the dialect from some Tunisian friends in Saudi, but I try to explain to him I don't understand him so we switch to Arabic Proper which neither of us is particularly good at, but it works.

With very profane vocabulary, he tells me he's visiting from Tunisia and his less than competent brother wasn't there to pick him up and the authorities couldn't let him go without a sponsor. He asks my story and if I had a phone or some cigarettes. I tell him I'm just a student trying to go home and that they had my phone and smokes and that I could use one too. He yells again, but this time he wakes the African man who offers him his phone. After the Tunisian finished yelling into the phone, the African goes to the window and knocks on it and a guard opens the door and lets him out. The Tunisian leaves shortly after that but I'm still here so I lie back down and continue remembering California.

Treize

We got to the agency and walked up the blue metal staircase in the back to the second floor where the office was. We walked in and saw a mix of Persian and Ottoman memorabilia and artifacts. The man greeted us but looked surprised like he didn't think we'd come, but there we were, and he seemed glad.

His name was Mohammad and his father was Iranian and his mother was Turkish but his loyalty leaned more towards Turkey. He's been in the country since he was a child during the Iranian Revolution and had always wanted to go back but he knew he couldn't. I told him my ancestry is Persian and my girlfriend was half Turkish and this pleased him like it's a good omen he recognized. We talked for about an hour about the motherland and living in the US after 9/11 and what Joe and I planned to do during our stay in the country. He offered us tea and taught us to keep a sugar cube between our teeth and sip the tea like they did in Iran.

We eventually got down to business as I signed the paperwork and had my license checked and photocopied and Joe paid for the car and insurance. We only had the car for five days, but the whole transaction cost upward of eight hundred dollars. But alas, everything checked through and the man walked us down the steps and showed us the Beast. It was the latest model white Toyota Corolla with a typical black plastic interior and an automatic transmission. For the money, Joe and I were a little bit disappointed, we expected something more memorable or special, but nonetheless, it was a car and we were free in Los Angeles for a week.

We thanked Mohammad for his kindness, hospitality, and help and promptly got underway. Joe had a new iPhone with the new Apple Maps app and I was the one with the license so by default, I drove and he navigated us directly to Venice Beach.

Driving down the big boulevards and avenues felt righteous and well deserved. We felt like we were in the opening scene of Entourage on our way to wreak socially semi-acceptable havoc. Joe noticed that we were crossing a traffic light from Hollywood to Santa Monica and that the signs called them both cities independent of one another. I suppose this is why we were in LA County, and not just the City of Angels. We found some street side parking for about seven dollars an hour. It blew our minds how much more expensive parking was compared to VT where an hour was for a quarter, and in Saudi where we could just park on a sidewalk for free and no legal consequence.

We walked around the famous Santa Monica pier at the end of Route 66. It was full of very attractive couples who we both knew were, like Charley Sheen would say, "winning." We took pictures of the Pacific Ocean. It was his first time seeing it and it may as well have been mine too. Unfortunately I had forgotten my camera in Virginia, so the only evidence we had of being in Cali were cell phone pictures and a lanyard from the seminar. This was a good thing, though, less fear of getting mugged and the pictures must always be vanilla and low quality enough to send to family.

We began walking toward Venice Beach and the scenery didn't change much. There was the sand beach to our left with the lifeguard shacks every couple of hundred yards and grass and extravagant small houses to our right. It felt like we were in San Andreas, the video game.

We eventually got to the commercial area and

it was filled with hotdog stands, street musicians performing, souvenir and low buck clothing stores, and on every block was a green cross representing a medical marijuana doctor. We stopped at the nearest one to ask about the process of getting a card, and the young lady in the lab coat, dressed in short summer clothes and almost entirely covered in tattoos told us we can't get one since we're from out of state. It was slightly demoralizing, but we decided to keep trying. The next couple of places were the same.

As we were turned down by the fourth place, a man with a sign approached us telling us his shop could help us out so we followed him. He took us to a "clinic" behind some building, it looked shady, but places like that are where laws are adjusted to accommodate the underprivileged.

The clinic was run by a group of Palestinians who were pleased that my grandmother is from the West Bank before the 1967 War. Joe didn't add that his mother is ethnically Jewish, and that may have been a good thing. We asked if they could help us and the lady said of course. She said she didn't need an ID and we could use the hotel as our address, and after filling the paper work, she let me see the Doctor.

I walked into his dim lit office and he

motioned with his hand for me to sit down. He looked like he was in his late fifties and his face was red and his voice was deep. In a short burst, he asked me what was wrong and I told him I had insomnia, a constant migraine, overwhelming stress, back pains, stomach problems, and as I was about to continue he puts his hands up like I had said enough. He pushed a button on his desk and the lady came back for me. The Doctor didn't seem to breath the whole time I was in there.

The lady asks if I'd like the prescription in paper form or if I paid forty dollars extra I could get a photo ID card. Joe and I decide the paper is better because it means he can go into a dispensary and buy some without photo ID. We tell the lady we only have eighty dollars left since the cab fare to the rental place and the car itself and parking were more expensive than we had anticipated and asked her if she'd take credit. These clinics and dispensaries only use untraceable cash and it cannot be handed from one person to another. In order to pay, you must put the cash on the counter and they must pick it up from the counter. There is absolutely no physical contact nor hand to hand exchange. She tells me the consultation alone costs sixty and the minimum three month prescription was another sixty. However since we're visitors from Home, she'd give me a year in paper form, as well as a nice little two inch pipe and some coupons for a couple local dispensaries. She was the greatest.

Neither Joe nor I remember much of the trip after that moment. We remember a couple of moments in Universal Studios, and even a snapshot in San Diego and Wiz was there, but we can't confirm. Wiz denies it ever happening with sarcasm and no real disclosure. The pictures were lost some time shortly after the trip.

We went back to Virginia after our first weed pilgrimage for two more weeks before moving to Baltimore. We felt cleansed and purified and grown and it was a great segue between the year at VT and the rest of our lives.

Quatroze

I woke up from the sound of the dark haired gate officer coming into the cell to ask how I'm doing. I tell her I've seen better days. She apologizes and says she knows I didn't do anything wrong and promises it'll all be alright and that I'll be out of here soon. I tell her I hope so. She walks out, her shift ended at least an hour ago. It's 10.00pm.

The Tunisian man comes back into the room but this time as silent as the night. He's limping, goes and sits on the bench opposite to the side of the room I'm at and lies down and disappears into his mind. I hear him sobbing but there's nothing I can do so I just sit and exist in the present. I'm trapped and afraid and helpless too.

A little while later, the fat man tells the officers to bring me in again. He cross checked my name with Interpol and found that my story checks out entirely. American Airlines was fined roughly twenty-five thousand Euros for this mistake. He tells me he has me booked on the next flight on Saudia back to Jeddah the following afternoon and that I should call my family again and tell them everything will be okay. We're waiting for a bus to come and take me to the hotel he mentioned earlier.

The officer in the room already has my cell phone and hands it to me and I call my family and tell them the good news. My dad asks if I knew which hotel it was and that I should shower and order pepper steak as room service and have it charged on the credit card he gave me. My mom says she's called several government agencies in Saudi and the embassy in France and they all say the French are just following protocol and there's nothing to be done, but I reassure her everything will be okay regardless. Lamees however, doesn't believe me and thinks my promise means nothing and that I'm just trying to calm her down. She demands that I see her as soon as I'm back home and I tell her I can't since I'm expecting my father to pick me up but I will see her once the dust settles.

The officer takes my phone once he sees me distressed trying to explain to her that this is real and that I haven't run away with someone in Paris. I thank him and he tells me she'll believe me once she sees me, not with words, but with his eyes. I know. He tells me it'll be a short while before we get moving.

He walks me back into the cell. Both times he opened the door, the Tunisian man flinches with hope or fear. I feel sorry for him. I don't know what's happened to him and what his story really is, but I hope everything will be okay with him as well.

I feel a little better about my situation knowing that I'll be home in less than a day. I worry about my parents and Lamees though. This must be one situation they never thought could happen. My parents will be fine once they see me and the report they'll give me, besides they've made the appropriate calls and have been reassured by people with more authority than me that everything will be okay.

Lamees on the other hand, the poor girl, has been waiting for this night for at least a month and waiting to see me for years. She's made plans for her family to spend the night at a beach resort telling them she's sick last minute and that they should enjoy themselves and take pictures. She doesn't know about the pendant or the other gifts I have for her and I know she's only mad because of how much she misses me and how built up our night was and how it just won't come to fruition.

I know not having my phone to constantly

reassure her is selfish and how much she needs me right now, but at times like this, I think selfishness is justified. I'll see her when I'm back after I've worked out what happened and paid my dues to my family for scaring them like this. I hope she'll understand. I know she will. She's a wonderful human and I'm lucky to have her in my life loving me like she does.

There is commotion outside as the clock approaches midnight. It's almost Christmas Eve and the officers are celebrating with champagne and chocolates. One of them comes into the cell and offers the Tunisian man and me some snacks to enjoy as well. The Tunisian doesn't want any, but I could use some sugar or caffeine. I ask if I can have a smoke somewhere, still no. The officer leaves and shuts the door again.

The jetlag is kicking in and I feel a boost of energy for no other apparent reason. If it's midnight here then it's 3.00pm in Wisconsin and I'd be just now returning from school. I hope I get some sleep in the hotel, my body is conflicted and doesn't know how it should feel. I'm energetic, but still ever so tired like when you've downed a Red Bull to counter the caffeine crash while studying late for an exam in the morning.

Quinze

The laughter has faded and it's much quieter now outside than it was a little while ago. I assume it's past midnight by maybe an hour or so. The Tunisian man sits up and asks me how I'm doing. He apologizes for his earlier behavior and when I ask what happened, he looks away indicating he doesn't want to talk about it. I tell him I'm fine and I was promised to go home tomorrow. He scoffs like he doesn't believe me or how naïve I am to trust the fat man. I'm a little worried by this, but how wrong could I be, really?

Even if they did want to punish me, it would make much more sense to just deport me than to keep me, if only for economic reasons. I don't know, though, this isn't a situation I learned about in school despite the many Poli-Sci courses I've taken. I'll be alright, though, I can feel it. Besides, I didn't do anything wrong and they know it.

A different officer than the ones I've met so far

comes into the room and tells us both to get up and follow him. The new shift has started and not even the fat man is in his office anymore. He takes us into the interrogation room and has us point out our belongings and to sign a forfeiture agreement saying that if we are carrying anything that is against French laws then not only do they keep all our belongings, but we face judicial repercussions. He has us patted down again one last time and we leave our stuff in the room.

We follow him down the long, dark hallway that leads to the staircase, but instead of getting off at the terminal, we continue climbing to the ground floor. I ask him where we're going and what time it is. He says Autobus and 2.20am. I'm glad the Tunisian man is coming as well.

We exit through an emergency door from the staircase and wait outside for the bus to arrive. It's freezing cold, windy, and raining. Good thing I'm wearing one of my two favorite sweaters, which I got as a birthday gift from one of my friends in Virginia. The Tunisian man is less fortunate. He forgot his jacket in the interrogation room and the officer wouldn't let him go get it. He's wearing a dark brown button up tee-shirt and khakis. I'm much more comfortable in my thick Under Armor sweatpants and Chucks. He's cleanly shaven with short hair, I usually let my hair grow in the Wisconsin winter as a last line of defense from the cold and wanted to shave when I got to Jeddah. I realize now how shady I look and I suppose it explains some of the hostility I've received while here.

The bus is a full sized, black Peugeot panel van with vinyl seats inside. It looks like a repurposed police van still carrying it's red and blue lights. It's scary but the officer gives us both reassuring pats on the back, gives the driver some documents, presumably our passports and case reports, and walks back into the building. I check my pocket to make sure I still have the corresponding case number ticket the fat man gave me earlier and the Tunisian does the same while he shivers in the cold.

The van's sliding door opens and the African man from earlier yells for us to quickly get in and away from the cold. I look at the Tunisian man and he gets in first, I follow. The van is toasty and warm like the heater has been on for a while. There are several other people with us including the driver and two officers sitting up front next to him. All three rows of passenger bench seats are now full. It's almost pitch black except the street lights from the front.

Everyone is quiet except one older man who is sitting right behind the driver laughing with the officers, telling jokes and anecdotes in French. He asks something and the driver responds. He then looks at the Tunisian man and me and introduces himself in Arabic as Michel. He's Lebanese and has been stuck at this airport for the past week. He tells us the staff are very friendly and kind and forgiving. The Tunisian man scoffs again, and the Michel laughs asking what he did to upset them. He doesn't respond.

I ask Michel about the hotel we're staying at and if I'll be able to shower, smoke, and who would pay for the pepper steak? Michel breaks into a hard laugh and explains my question to the officers and they laugh too. He tells me that there is no hotel, just the housing complex, and yes, I can shower, not that I'd want to there, and I can smoke if I had my own smokes. Oh boy.

The ride is quiet after that as morale drops among the passengers. Even Merry Michel goes silent and looks straight ahead. It's no longer cold, but I still feel the Tunisian man shivering. I feel a little cold inside too like my bones are hollowed and filled with ice. I'm dehydrated and hungry as well, and yet I feel the need to use the bathroom. I don't know where we are or where we're going. I don't know how long we'll really be there and what'll happen next. I don't have my phone or my smokes or any of my documents. I am an anonymous body, one of many, cold, trapped, alone, and afraid. However, I remember what the shuttle driver told me about being somewhere I don't speak the language, and I feel a little more at ease about it all.

Seize

It is still dark the rain got worse as we get off the van. The building is three stories high, does not have more than two windows per floor and they're all barred up. There is a big fence around it topped with barbed wire. The florescent lights on the outside flickers in the rain. I'd just flown in from Chicago but this building looms over me more so than any sky scraper I'd ever stepped into. It swallows me with such complete anonymity that even I hardly knew I was there, not that it matters.

The officers motion for me to walk into a bright, cramped and crowded room where halfway into it there is a desk with people wearing high visibility vests over grey sweatshirts. They have breathing masks and nylon gloves on. They are more organized and are in control of registration and administration.

A man in a mask hands me a clipboard and some paperwork that's written in French, Hmong, bad Arabic, Spanish, and English. I write in my name, passport details, itinerary, and case number. It is verified on a computer and the man gives my officer escort keys to my room, a receipt, and instructions in French. He wishes me a merry Christmas and I thank him.

The officer then leads me down a long orange colored hall, humid with the scent of human sweat from the radiators keeping the temperature tolerable. It is a truly grim place to be and the fact that I still don't quite understand why or how I got here brings upon my imagination the worst. Is this how it ends? Is this the hotel in which I can order the pepper steak my father promised to comfort me with or is this where I will be indefinitely until I become just another number on some report and then I die?

Not knowing where I am, my nearest guess is a refugee detention camp like the ones I hear about on the news in Australia and Greece where the captives are assaulted by the captors and other captives who may have lost their minds since they were forced out of their homes.

Before losing their identity and dignity, they lost their lives and their loved ones. They used to be doctors and engineers and lawyers and business owners and accountants. They watched TV and enjoyed good food and had hopes for an ordinary future of stability and love and happiness. Those days are gone, now they strive for what they can get, which can be summarized as Hope.

Since they are so used to traveling, they are much more accustomed to the honesty and naturalism I noticed in O'Hare. They do not fear being judged nor do they care much for civility and common decency, however they might have the most common sense. Scuffing down whatever they could get their hands on while still flapping like a fish out of water. Vultures at on the wrong end of the food chain, bottom feeders and tonight I am a dead diver.

Then it dawned on me. These dirty people aren't just the deranged products of history in the making; they just haven't showered in a while. They are real normal people whom have had strings of unfortunate events, who had lost their livelihoods and were forced away from the luxuries of comfort and convenience. They are regular people whose lives were lost in translation in a country that does not need to accommodate more of the same normality. Whatever mind they lost, can be found along the way from where they were to where they are now. It's a morbid thought, but as far as I'm concerned, I have come to join them. The question now is, since I've already been stripped from my personhood, do I give in and give the authorities my own mind as well, do I try to keep it as long as I can, or do I try to escape, and if so, how?

I think back to the Lebanese man and how easy and comfortable he seemed. The Tunisian man is the exact opposite, broken and cold. The African man didn't get off the bus with us, maybe he goes to another facility. I wish I were more like the Lebanese man, I wish I spoke the language and could be more social. He's been here for at least a week, I imagine that was an understatement, but he seems fine. I'll think about my next course of action if they keep me from the flight tomorrow. But for now, I just want to rest.

Dix-Sept

The guard walks me up some stairs at the end of the hall. The staircase is painted a sort of pastel teal that looks easy to wear and restore. The steps are metal, covered with light colored vinyl tiles and the rail is steel painted in the same teal. We climb one flight of stairs to the second floor as the top floor is for the officers and their offices.

Directly to my right is another organizers' office. This time the lady gives me a paper to sign saying that I'm not contagious like with Ebola or something. She, too, is armored in medical protection. She tells the officer he may leave now and hands me the key he gave her as well as a rations bag with some chocolates, chips, a couple of drinking water cups and tuna similar to that given in the cell from earlier. She tells me to find my room and to be up and ready to leave at 6.30am. It's 3.00am now. I don't have time to properly rest.

Room 10, room 11, room 12, room 14, it's close

to the office and the stair case, that's convenient. It has a sink and mirror and some storage. It has two beds and I don't have a roommate. The bathrooms are in the hall, meaning that I can leave my room whenever I please, which was good news, I suppose. Now to figure out the smoking policy and find some cigs.

Dix-Huit

I don't have anything with me to worry about getting stolen. Matter of fact, aside from the clothes I'm wearing, all I have with me are the keys to my room that only locks from the outside anyway, and the bag of snacks. I wash my face in the room and head out looking to discover what this place is really about and whether or not I actually can finally have a smoke.

As far as I can tell, it's a dormitory for people who, like me, aren't allowed to stay at the airport or leave it. It's nicer than I had initially thought it would be, but that's not saying much. Although the lights are all on, it still feels very dark. I walk out the door and I'm immediately surprised to find all the life I didn't notice coming in. I suppose now that the pressure is off and I have some freedom to move about, my vision is broader than just on myself and where I'm going. There are people all over the place, but nobody notices me.

I see people of all races and tongues, clothed in all sorts of fabrics and colors. It doesn't smell as horrid as I thought it would, or maybe I smell as just bad as the building does. I see Africans speaking different languages, mostly French, though. I recognize someone speaking Swahili from a Kenyan friend who'd talk on the phone with his mother for an hour every time we met promising her we won't do anything stupid and that she shouldn't worry. There may be at least thirty black people here, but they aren't a majority.

There is a group of about fifteen light skinned people of all ages huddled up around an old couple sitting on chairs in a corner. Could this be one family? They look similar enough, and there are three identifiable generations. It looks like the grandparents, a few adult parents holding a bunch of half asleep children. The old man is telling a story which I could only presume to be of the birth of Christ, the lady next to him is caressing one of the children and the young adults are gathered listening to find inspiration within their predicament. I don't understand the language, however they look Caucasian, possibly from Armenia or Georgia.

One of the rooms has a Kurdish flag hanging on the door. I knock on it hoping to find someone who speaks Arabic since so far nobody seems to speak English. A young girl opens the door, not older than twelve, maybe, so I ask her for her name and if there's anyone else around her. An older lady jumps out of bed, yelling in neither Arabic nor French nor English, grabs the girl and slams the door. Her face was full of scars like acid burns and the fear of someone who's seen some bad days. I hope she doesn't think I had any wicked intentions. I suppose looking like I do and the context of the place we're in doesn't help. I hope I didn't wake them, I just now realize how late it is.

I keep walking until I eventually find a bathroom and open the door. I close the door the second the stench hits me like a stab on the inside of my nose. I no longer really need to use the bathroom. It can wait until I'm back at the airport.

I hear a burst of loud laughing and I turn around and see the Tunisian man with some other people in a room across from me. They saw me get grossed out and found light in it. The Tunisian man calls on me to join them. I'm glad he looks better bundled up in a blanket to undo the cold he's experienced earlier. I have a couple of hours to kill and nothing better to do, I may as well.

Dix-Nuef

There are five guys beside the Tunisian man in the room. Each with his own history and reason for being here. They're all speaking different dialects of Arabic with a little French tossed in here and there. It's a curious sight seeing them all in this room together.

The Tunisian man introduces me as Saudi and explains to me that my name is irrelevant here, and I will be identified by my nationality, which is the only thing the French see in me anyway. He points out each of the guys in the room and introduces them by their former nationalities as well. He tells me these people no longer adhere to any nation. That they've either run away from their homes or no longer have homes at all to run from. Based on the countries he mentions, I'm not the least bit surprised by this, and for some reason, no longer afraid.

The way they laugh indicates some sense of camaraderie almost a brotherhood between those to whom borders are just lines on the ground. When you don't have anything to lose you are free. They are all trapped here for the time being, but they are free men. To them, this is just another waypoint along the way. There is food and shelter and it'll determine where they go next. I ask their stories.

Vingt

Egypt One tells me he was at Tahrir Square during the January Revolution that overthrew Mubarak. He recalls with vivid detail camping over night and chanting that the people demand the fall of the regime. He says it was all peaceful and that the protesters would march at night and clean up in the morning. He says it was cathartic and beautiful and organized, at least until the government blacked out all media and the internet. He says the protests only turned into clashes after the authorities interfered violently, but it was never their intention.

He's been shot at with what the news claimed were rubber bullets, but he describes that they were regular shotgun rounds with a thin layer of rubber that are supposed to render them non-lethal. He says a man next to him who was throwing rocks at troops was shot in the eye and died on the spot. While telling the story, he seems shell shocked even though it's been close to three years.

He says it seemed worth it until entire families started losing their homes or were killed during "random police sweeps" throughout the process. He recalls specifically one night when a big black van rushed through a crowd over the Lion bridge across the Nile while snipers were raining down live ammunition and tear gas. His younger sister was run over that night on that bridge. She was only thirteen. The van was heading into the US embassy in Cairo and it was made clear whose side the Obama administration was really on, in spite of his many press conferences urging Mubarak to step down in the name of "Democracy."

He left Egypt shortly after, flying to Jordan and walking through Syria before the war erupted toward Turkey where he was held by a NATO check point. He was shipped to France for processing and has been in this facility since. They promise to revisit his case once a month but he says he's lost hope and just wants to go back to how things were.

I ask him how he felt when Morsi took power. He was elated and prayed thanks to God like he's never done before. He says the euphoria of knowing political justice was to be served was overwhelming and that the brothers in Palestine deserved an Egyptian ally who'd protect them and provide for them. He says it gave him hope of returning to an Egypt that was much less corrupt and looked forward to an optimistic future with opportunity for all. He remarks that it is a shame that some Egyptians are much more into porn than justice and that they didn't deserve what Morsi and the Brotherhood had in store. With a nihilistic sense of irony, he says it's all written.

Vingt-et-Un

Egypt Two, who looks even younger than me, is displeased by this exchange of sympathy toward Morsi. It's obvious he was in the opposing camp claiming the Brotherhood is a terrorist organization bent on destroying what's left of the already crippled Egyptian economy in efforts to support a losing front in the Palestine-Israel conflict. He says Morsi cracked down on more than just porn, he was going to enforce Sharia Law like in Saudi and make women cover up their faces and ban free media among other things. His argument that in the compromise between political justice and social justice, the happiness people feel due to freedom is more important than bad people rotting in jail for their corruption and cronyism.

I ask him about the election and Morsi winning a majority and he dismisses it saying the Brotherhood rigged the whole thing. He doesn't know a single person who voted for Morsi yet when the results were published, they said his entire neighborhood voted in that direction. A second revolution was necessary to bring back whatever order existed under Mubarak. However awful that regime was, at least there was a regime.

So I ask him for his thoughts on Sisi. He says he's god-awful and a sellout, but the people were aware of that going in. They knew he was just a replacement for Mubarak as far as the oligarchy and the country's allies are concerned. Sisi could be a Jew for all he cared, but as long as he wasn't a Brotherhoodist, he's okay. Egypt One interrupts saying Sisi is a Jew, his mother is anyway, and a debate rages between them.

I cut them off asking Egypt Two why he's here if Sisi was so great. He says he wishes he were home but he doesn't have one to go back to. He ran away under Morsi before the second revolution. His father was a journalist who was apprehended by Brotherhood thugs for pointing out inconsistencies in the drafts of the new constitution. He was executed without word getting out and his remains were burned.

I get goose bumps as I see these two people fight over whose relative's death was most heartbreaking. They both lived in the same city under the same conditions most of their lives. They both fought opposite sides of the same war. They both lost that war. Now, they both share a room with their enemy; identified as one, only by the place they hate the most. Humiliated and dehumanized, they will remain in this facility indefinitely. Egypt Two storms out of the room with tears in his eyes and Egypt One follows to console him.

Vingt-Deux

There are two men left in the room beside the Tunisian man and me; I suppose, I should call him Tunis from now on. One of them offers me a Kit-Kat and I refuse saying I got my own and offer him some of the chips I'm eating. He tells me he's Libya.

His story is similar to that of the Egyptians', however slightly different. He was in the town neighboring Ben Ghazi where the US embassy was attacked and Gaddafi was killed. He didn't want to participate in the revolution calling the whole Arab Spring an attempt by the West to disorganize and divide the Middle East and North Africa so that they would have uncontested access to our natural resources and exploit us. He believed Gaddafi was a jackass but at least he loved his country and his people more so than the next guy.

He says wars aren't about dictators and freedom, they are never about people's rights to choose their own destiny. War is about resources, in this case blood for barrels and he wanted none of it. He asks me if I knew what the American troops were doing in Libya, I tell him I only know they're trying to fight ISIL. He laughs and says yes, but not to protect the people, just the oil. He says the country has completely collapsed over the course of the past couple of years with the exception of the oil industry. The only stability comes under BP and Shell logos and that's the only place the military exists in full force. He says that was evidence enough to convince him to leave, and so he did.

He escaped by boat heading to Algeria but the boat was caught by pirates and held for ransom. The French Navy rescued them and flew the passengers without a real destination to various parts of the European Union as asylum. He's been here for the past eight months and has four months to go before he is granted freedom.

I ask him about his family and friends, he says he was the only son and moved out of his father's house as a teenager to become a farmer due to economic reasons and his father took offense to it and cut him off entirely. He hasn't had family for the better part of two decades and doesn't intend on trying to find them. He also doesn't really have friends back home, saying the people around him here are the only friends

and family he'll ever care about, but he knows
the minute he's out even this life is over and
he'll start anew. I tell him I hope it all works out.
He sighs and tells me he does too.

Vingt-Trois

A bell rings softly from an overhead speaker in all the rooms and the men quickly get up and tell me to follow them. Apparently it rings every two hours indicating that the yard door is open for fresh air and people often use the fifteen minutes either to exercise or to smoke. Tunis and I are glad Libya has a few spare cigarettes he offers us and we accept with gratitude. They're harsh on the throat and they taste horrible, but the buzz is sufficient and we both needed it after such a long day.

The rain has stopped but it's still very cold and cloudy. It's dark and I can't see any lights from over the fence. I hear airplanes take off and land so the airport's nearby, but not by much. I ask Libya what this place is and he says it's Heaven. It's where good people go when their lives back home are over. The bad people go to jail or worse, and although here we're not free, at least we're not punished, and at the end of the day, it's better than being caught in war and watching people you love die as a part of someone else's politics. I ask him once more what this place is hoping he'd be a little more technical and he gives me a look like he's curious yet annoyed at my questioning. I get the hint and don't ask again. A different bell rings indicating time's up. It's 4.15am.

Vingt-Quatre

We walk back up to the room to find someone I haven't met yet. Libya tells me this is Bahrain. He escaped the crackdown on Shiites in 2012 but Bahrain interrupts him telling him it's not my business, as a Saudi, to know these things, after all, it was Saudi who led that effort. Libya realizes this whole time I was just listening and didn't tell my story so he asks me as if to prove to him I'm not a spy of some sort.

Knowing there's no way out of this but to talk, I begin telling my lame story to try to defuse the hostile tension. I start by reassuring them I'm no spy, just a student trying to go home to my lover but had a slight mix up along the way. I tell them about Madison and Kansas and Virginia and how the struggle as a person of color in the US may not always be life or death, unless you're black, but the fear is still real. I try not to over dramatize my experience since I know whatever I've been through does not come close to what they've lived.

I used to see a physiotherapist in Kansas because I had back problems and on my first visit he asked me if we had medicine in the Middle East. I asked him if he knew who Avicenna was and he said of course. I told him he was an Arab Muslim and the doctor seemed shocked, a little disappointed, and slightly offended. The next appointment I had, I went dressed in my nicest Armani shirt and a turban and the staff at the clinic started talking to me differently like I didn't understand them the first time. I didn't go back to that clinic after that.

On my way home that day I had the radio in the truck blasting whatever was playing, being Kansas it was Country, and I got hailed over to the side of the road by a man in a Toyota Prius. My first thought was that he was either going to tell me something's wrong with the car or yell at me for driving a big gas guzzler. I was wrong. He yelled at me to go back to my fucking country since I'm a dirty sand nigger. I laughed at his face asking how his grand pappy would feel if he knew his piece of shit grandson drove a Japanese car. He sped off. I left Kansas a week later.

I tell them about the schools I've attended and the friends I've made and my family's support and it seems like they're relieved by my stories.

It's almost like I'm a window to the good life that they, ever so badly, needed to look through. They've been running from their past for so long, it's almost like they've lost sight of where they're heading and I help redirect their gazes and goals.

I tell Bahrain that a couple of my closest Saudi friends were Shiite, one from Jeddah, and one from Qatif. I tell him I'm somewhat aware of how horribly Shiites are treated and viewed in the public eye. It's akin to the anti-Semitism in Europe, or anti-Catholicism in the US before Kennedy became president. I tell him my ancestry is Persian and I have family all across the gulf who are Shiite and I wish them no harm. I tell them I'm a pacifist and how I disapprove of all the conflicts going on and I wish people would just sit down and talk things out. We can go a long way with diplomacy.

I tell them I understand how I can come off as an insider trying to get them in trouble, but the fact is I was more afraid of them coming in than they ever should be of me. Libya laughs pointing at how I look ready to win any fight I get into. I tell him my hair and beard are just for warmth and that under this sweater there are no muscles, just a body shaped by more pizza than the average person has in a lifetime. Ultimately,

97

however different our stories are, right now, we're all in the same place.

I can see him warm up to me and I hope he truly believes how honest and sincere I'm being. Libya looks to Bahrain and asks what he's thinking. With little hesitation, he lets out a sigh and agrees to tell me his story.

Vingt-Cinq

He was born and raised a devout Shiite in a Manama outskirt to a moderate family. He went to school studying the typical indoctrinating system saying Shiites are bad and Salafi Sunnis were the only good Muslims but his family taught him it wasn't true. They often looked to Iran's grand mufti for guidance as did all the other Shiites in the area and would find solace in the collective struggle they had. He says he didn't mind being the underdog or be labeled an infidel and outcast because he didn't feel it. Bahrain is a very small country, smaller than most cities and predominantly Shiite, so even his friends at school couldn't tell they were "oppressed."

In high school while his parents expected him to get a girlfriend, he found it very difficult and was not attracted to any girls. Every time he'd ask one out he found that what they had in common didn't fit the descriptions of what his friends had in common with their girlfriends, but he would rather have these girls as just friends. I realized what he was eluding to and Libya confirmed. Bahrain is gay and I understood how difficult it must have been for him.

Libya holds him by the shoulder and looks at me with the look of a wild cat protecting her young and tells me this is a safe place and if I even think of changing that I will reap what I sew. I tell him not to worry, I've marched at Pride Parades in Madison and I've fought where I could for equality and coexistence and reconciliation. I am an ally if ever there was one. Both he and Bahrain nod with vague approval.

Bahrain continues saying what was on the news was taken at face value, just as Television programming, it was entertainment. He says his mother wanted to leave when tensions rose but his father refused saying they had as much a right to stay as their Sunni counterparts. He was very patriotic and even volunteered in the army to fight Saddam Hussein when he invaded Kuwait. He said leaving goes against everything he stood for, everything he fought for, and he refused to budge.

It wasn't until the Sunnis started bombing Shiite mosques all around the Gulf that his father realized his nationalism meant nothing to the status quo. Against the family's wishes, Bahrain's father marched and protested for a freedom and equality in the country. He didn't want to topple the monarchy nor change it, he just wanted representation and recognition for his efforts. He was arrested and taken away as if erased from the face of the earth.

Bahrain came out to his mother that week and she disowned him, as if losing his father and the safety at home wasn't enough. He left the country through Qatar and somehow found himself backpacking through Europe. He is no longer a Muslim; all his religion did was bring him grief, and now he has a family and is safe and happy.

Vingt-Six

The whole night there was a man in the room with us who didn't speak a word. I ask Libya who he is and if there's something wrong with him. He says with a smile on his face that's Belgium. He's not really from there, but just his passport. He can't talk because his tongue was cut out by some mafia in Macao. He's quite the trouble maker, and very funny.

He's actually Tunisian and when the Arab Spring first happened, he took advantage of the opportunity and flew out to the Far East. He was able to get a counterfeit Belgian passport from Indonesia, thinking it was some obscure former Soviet, Eastern European country, as opposed to the capitol of the EU. He's seen almost every country east of India with that passport and was intending on seeing the world.

He was flying from Papua New Guinea to Iceland through Paris thinking he can just walk through security like he's been doing since he got the passport. Obviously, he got caught and has been here for the past three months pleading with the courts to let him stay. His next hearing is in a week, or in his case, reading. As smart as he is, he's a total idiot, Libya says and Belgium flips him off. We all laugh.

He knows a number of verbal languages, it's unfortunate he can't speak though. So he learned sign language and taught it to a select few people here including Libya and Bahrain, if only to tell jokes.

In all seriousness, though, it's been tough for him to cope without being able to talk, he can hear, however, and has heard the whole night's conversation. He signs to Libya that he'd like him to translate a story for Tunis and me, since we're new here.

As he begins to sign, Bahrain starts giggling like he knows the story. Libya is watching intently, translating obscure facts and details to describe the setting. He's telling us about his second to last night in Thailand.

It was a hot and humid day and he was high on some opiates with a lover he's rented. They went out on a boat to watch the sunset. As they were kissing, things escalated. The hooker reached into his pants began touching him so he lifted her skirt. He stops for effect and signals to Libya, who punches Tunis in the groin exclaiming, that's why they call it Bangkok! Bahrain burst out laughing. Belgium started laughing too, but also yells at Libya for punching too hard.

I'm just shocked that Belgium can speak! He looks at me and says he didn't get his tongue cut out. Well, obviously. Tunis is on the floor in agony and Libya explains that he wasn't cool enough to deserve a lighter hit.

I ask Belgium why he lied, and he says because he can. He explains that there's no point being in this place if you can't tell a joke. Life's too depressing as is.

Vingt-Sept

The bell rings again. It's 6.00am already. Libya and Belgium carry Tunis and put him on a bed to rest after that blow. They ask me if I'd like another cigarette and I gladly accept.

While downstairs, I tell them I have to leave soon. They look at me with mixed feelings like we've become good friends and here I am off to leave them. I tell them it's been a long couple of days and although I can't wait to get home and rest, if the worst happens and I'm forced to stay a little longer, I won't be afraid and I know I'm welcome here. We smoke and laugh and joke about the horrors of this place and other places. I thank them for the wonderful night and promise never to forget them.

I go directly back to my room this time and wash my face again. I lie down for a couple of minutes and someone knocks on my door. It's the officer who brought me up here a few hours ago. He points at his watch and I follow him. We pick up a folder from the office where I signed the illness form and go to the dining hall for breakfast.

There's nothing appetizing, but I do see all the guys from the night, except Tunis. I'm not allowed to talk with them now and they understand. We wave to each other, I grab a coffee, and the officer takes me downstairs where the van from earlier is waiting. The African man and Michel are also there. I think I'm going home.

Vingt-Huit

As I come to leave the building I get a strange feeling of nostalgia and sorrow. It's is bizarre to think that just a few hours ago I felt like I would die in this place, nameless, my story unheard, and my legacy unsung. Now I feel like of all the places I've ever been to, this has been the most authentic and novel experience I've ever had. The people, the most honest and genuine. None of them have done anything objectively wrong either, and yet here they all are, in this building together as if their destinies have much more in store for them but none of them know it yet.

As terrified as I was walking in, not for a second was I afraid since leaving the room to walk around. If anything, I felt privileged and fortunate to have come from such a stable and safe place, to know I will be leaving soon, and to know that there is little for me ever to fear again. It's inspiring how the people I've met hold themselves in this circumstance with such poise and strength. The fraternal aura that exists between them is familiar and reminds me of Virginia. Their acceptance of fate is somewhat nihilistic like the negative part of an existential crisis, but the bond between them keeps them grounded and the support and humanist love they have for one another keeps them sane. Although they didn't do anything wrong either, here they are, in most cases, indefinitely.

The building no longer seems frightening in the morning light. It is grey with blue accents. It feels inflated and innocuous, like a bloated beer belly after a long game night with friends. It isn't anything more than it is, a housing facility for those who need one. It is what it is, and it's unashamedly that.

Destiny and Fate have always had a strong effect on me. I'm not very religious but I am spiritual enough to believe in a bigger picture; a grand design of some sorts. They have taken me to the ends of the earth to some people. They have touched my life at a very young age and have never left me. Even in my darkest moments, I always knew that the end of my story on this planet is at my death and therefore I've kept my head up looking for the next adventure.

The people I've met tonight manifest that to its extreme. They have experienced much worse than my lowest points. They've lost their homes and families and livelihoods and even their identities, but they soldier on like they know tomorrow will be better. Even if there's no sign of improvement, there is always space for Hope.

I want to have that sort of faith in Hope. That fierce fearlessness. That security in my vulnerability. That calmness in moments of calamity. What I've learned from the most conventionally feared segment of the global society is absolute humanity, humility, empathy, and compassion. I have never felt love like this and I hope I get to show it and share it with the world.

Vingt-Neuf

It's early in the morning and the ride was noticeably quiet. I ask Michel how his night went, but he's silent, barely awake. It seems as though he's either used to this routine, has partied too much, or too little. In either case, I lean back into my seat and quiet down too. I still can't see where we are or where we're going. It's frigid and foggy, typical for a December morning after a cold rainy night. However the drive to the airport isn't nearly as long as it seemed earlier and we arrive before I expected.

We drop off the African man, escorted with one of the officers in the van and continue a half minute forward to another entrance where this time I get off with my own escort. Michel is still in the van sleeping, I hope his situation works out.

The officer is tall, white, blue eyed and has dark hair. He's dressed in dark cargo pants tucked into military boots, a white shirt, bulletproof vest and a raincoat. He's clean

shaven, fit, and looks very professional. This is
how they all dressed, but only now do I start
notice the details. He's very lightly armed yet
very nonthreatening and I realize he's just
another human fulfilling a different role in this
organic, mechanical community. He's a white
blood cell if ever a human was one.

He has a folder in his hand which I can only
hope is my case details and passport. He guides
me through an underground labyrinth I don't
recognize. I hope we're going to the terminal,
but it's still only 7.00am and my trip isn't until
1.00pm. My hands and face are cold, but the rest
of me is covered with thick cotton and polyester.
The hallway is dark except for some spotlights
centered on the ceiling every few feet. I'm not
afraid or worried or anything, I'm tired and cold
and I just want to sit down.

We get to a staircase and climb half a floor to
find a door we walk through. We are inside the
airport, but I don't recognize where exactly. I ask
if I'm free to go, he shakes his head and points at
his watch that it's still too early. I remember he
still has my papers, and the airport still has my
bags and things. So I follow him a bit more and
we walk through a restricted access door similar
to last night's but not the same. This was behind
some vending machines and didn't lead to a

staircase or a hall.

Behind the door was a little police suite composed of an office room, a kitchenette, and behind a wall, a barred up jail cell. The officer at the desk calls me over and hands me my bag and the checklist from yesterday and tells me to go through and make sure everything is there. I do and it all checks out. I pull out Cosmos by Carl Sagan, the book I promised myself I'd read a little more from during the trip and I ask if it's okay for me to keep it with me during the wait since they won't let me have my bag quite yet. The man agrees and tells me to go sit in the cell.

It's a quiet morning and two of the four officers including my escort leave the office to go do their rounds or get coffee or whatever they do at this time. I'm alone on a metal bench in the cell and they left the bar door open. They all know I did nothing wrong and that I'm no threat to their safety or anyone else's. I'm a low priority anonymous suspect of no crime at all and I appreciate this trust.

I look at the book in my hand and flip through it. I bought it in DC the week my mom and sister came to visit, as well as another book I had finished that week. I never quite got to finishing this book as it is extremely dense with information and is so elegantly written that I never felt either too hooked nor too bored to continue. I open up to the bookmark I left. It's a thin sheet of mahogany with a leaf carved into it. I bought a bunch of these the same week I bought the books. It's beautiful and handmade and expensive and I like it almost as much as I like the book I use it for.

I try to read but my sight can't pass the first words. I'm far too emotionally overwhelmed and physically exhausted. I put the book down on the bench as a pillow and lay on my back. I have a few hours to go, I may as well nap a little.

Trente

As I lay wide eyed hoping to catch some sleep, I notice the walls in the suite are all bare concrete. The bars and the bench are brushed steel and like the other cell, there is no faux ceiling to hide the building's infrastructure. I realize there is far too much going on in my head right now to really, even for a minute, get some rest. I sit up and reflect on everything that's happened over the past thirty hours. It's only been that long, or thereabout, since we boarded in Chicago.

I remember a theory an old and wise friend of mine in Madison told me. He said that the city is build on an isthmus that was considered sacred land by the natives who lived there before the white man came. It was a place that demanded pilgrimage and to a lot of people it seemed to have its own spirit. He told me that nobody ever goes to Madison unless it invited them first, and though they may leave temporarily, they will never leave permanently until it is done with them.

The land changes the person, it cleanses them and it births them anew. It manifests itself in whatever form the person needs to listen; so as a person, or a place, or a thing, or an experience. Maybe, it can change a person even after they've left or while they are somewhere else. In any case, for some reason, I remember the way he told me that life, locations, people, even the weather, are much more to one's consciousness than just the background to one's life.

I wonder if after all of this I'll ever be able to go back to Madison, to my truck, to the college, to my friends. I wonder if I'll even be allowed to fly out of Saudi again or if I'll be put on some no-fly list or something. As far as I know, everything's fine and I did nothing wrong, but neither did any of the people I met last night.

I wonder what happened to that Kurdish woman that gave her that scar on her face. Why there was an entire family there and how long they've been stuck. I wonder what those parents tell their children. I wonder why there were so many French speaking Africans. One would think they'd be a priority to enter France since their lands couldn't deny the French entering during the Colonial Era. I wonder if Tunis ever got up after that blow and if he'll ever meet his brother. I wonder how many stories I heard were true and how many made up. There's no real reason to make up anything, but still I wonder.

Fate seems to have brought all those people to that facility for some reason. It has taken me there too, and yet I'm out and hopefully on my way home, it's just a couple more hours and I'll know for sure, but nevertheless, what could be the meaning of all this. I wonder.

Trente-et-Un

Before I know it, an officer comes to this side of the wall from the office and tells me it's already 10.00am and it's time to go to the terminal. The flight doesn't depart until 1.00pm, why go so early? He says something but I don't understand, I assume it's just protocol, or they, like me, just want to get this over with.

I follow him to the desk to grab my backpack. I put the book back in it. They make me sign a release form and hand my escort a copy of it and he puts it in the folder that's been following me since the fat man's office, and we head off out of the suite.

He tells me to walk beside him, and that he won't use the hand cuffs, I'm a little relieved and simultaneously disappointed, I think. But it's still clear that he's escorting me as opposed to helping me. We walk toward my gate and the terminal is massive with windows from the ceiling to the ground. The natural light feels liberating and fresh and underappreciated by everyone there.

He tells me to have a seat and sits next to me a little farther away from everyone else in the waiting area. We're facing the gate and so I notice all the Saudis staring at me and whispering to the people they are with, obviously gossiping and curious. It is an unfortunate trait prevalent in my people, and a disgusting one at that. I do however still look scary and unshaven, so I would understand any discomfort or hesitation from anyone to get on the plane with me even though I'm still uncuffed.

We sit in silence and wait until it's about 11.30am and the officer stands and takes me with him to the desk at the gate and hands the man there some papers. He looks through them and nods. He then opens the door to the jet way and the officer and I walk to the plane. Once there, he asks the flight attendant to speak with the captain and to have me seated. The flight attendant is a little stiff and walks me to the very last row on the plane and gives me the aisle seat.

I ask him about the folder in the officer's hand, but he just looks at me, appalled I'd disgrace him with verbal communication, tells me not to move, and walks away. I put on my seatbelt and wait for boarding to start.

It isn't long before the plane starts filling up, front to back, like Saudia has finally implemented Zone seating. A little later, my row mates finally arrive and take the window and middle seats. I almost ask if I can switch with the man next to the window, but choose not to annoy Mr. Hard-Ass Flight-Attendant, however the man in the middle asks me if I would switch with a third friend of theirs who's sitting elsewhere on the plane. If it were any other day, I likely would've accepted, but choose to refrain telling him I really can't, and immediately fall asleep.

Trente-Deux

The flight ends without a hitch or a hiccup. I wake up as we land in Jeddah and everybody gets off the plane. The flight attendant comes to me and tells me just as an officer in France escorted me on, I will need an officer to escort me off. I ask to speak with the captain and he reluctantly agrees.

The captain comes with the folder in his hand and asks me what's going on and what all of this is about. I explain very plainly to him that there was a simple mix up in Paris and that I didn't do anything wrong. He asks me if it's my papers he has in his hands, and I tell him I hope so, I haven't touched my passport since the gate officer took it from me in front of the Domestic Flights terminal.

He opens the folder and asks me for my name and date of birth, and I tell him and confirm with him it really is my passport. He asks me what I do for a living and I tell him I'm an international student just trying to go home for the winter and he can see my visa and stamps in the passport.

He looks puzzled as if he's never had to do this before, and I'm sure it's he hasn't, but he gives me the folder and looks me straight in the eye and says, "As captain of this ship, it is by my authority that you are free to go."

Fin.